Keeping

hools

Kate Purdie

WAYLAND

Published in 2013 by Wayland
Copyright © Wayland 2013

Wayland, 338 Euston Road, London NW1 3BH
Wayland Australia, Level 17/207 Kent Street, Sydney, NSW 2000

All rights reserved.

Produced for Wayland by Calcium
Design: Nick Leggett and Paul Myerscough
Editor: Sarah Eason
Picture research: Maria Joannou
Consultant: Sue Beck, BSc, Msc
Commissioning Editor for Wayland: Jennifer Sanderson

Acknowledgements

The publisher would like to thank the following for permission to reproduce photographs:
Alamy Images: Jim Lane 24, Mediablitzimages (UK) Limited/Martin Lee 14; Corbis: Image100 16,
17, Strauss/Curtis 25; Getty Images: The Image Bank/Darren Robb 23; Istockphoto: Miquel Munill
28bc, Plainview 28b, Alberto Pomares 20, Anthony Rosenberg 8, Thomas Vogel 28c;
Photolibrary: Flirt Collection/Jutta Klee 5; Science Photo Library: Dr P.Marazzi 15; Shutterstock: 12,
Aga & Miko (arsat) 18, Tiplyashin Anatoly 1, 19, Anyka 13, David Davis 26, Mandy Godbehear 9,
Ramzi Hachicho 11, David Hughes 27, IRA 6, Monkey Business Images 21, Margot Petrowski 7,
Jason Stitt 4, Mark Stout Photography 22, Makarova Tatiana 10. Cover: Getty Images/The Image
Bank/Darren Robb.

British Library Cataloguing in Publication Data
Purdie, Kate
Keeping clean. - (Being healthy, feeling great)
1. Hygiene - Juvenile literature
I. Title
613.4

ISBN: 978 0 7502 7148 6

2 4 6 8 10 9 7 5 3 1

Printed in China

Wayland is a division of Hachette Children's Books, an Hachette UK company.

www.hachette.co.uk

The website addresses (URLs) included in this book were valid at the time of going to press.
However, because of the nature of the Internet, it is possible that some addresses may have
changed, or sites may have changed or closed down since publication. While the author and
Publisher regret any inconvenience this may cause the readers, no responsibility for any such
changes can be accepted by either the author or the Publisher.

What is personal hygiene?

Personal hygiene is all about looking after yourself, and keeping yourself clean and healthy. It is mainly about taking good care of your body and the clothes and shoes you wear. Personal hygiene also involves keeping everyday items, such as computer keyboards, free of dirt, so you do not pick up germs that can make you ill.

Everyone likes to look and feel as good as they can and personal hygiene is a big part of this. It helps you to feel more confident because you know that you are clean and looking your best.

Other benefits

Good personal hygiene also helps to protect your body from illness and infection. If you did not wash, bacteria would grow on your skin. Bacteria can cause spots and spread disease. They can make your body a bit smelly, too. If you do not wash your hands after going to the toilet, you could get a bug that could make you very ill indeed.

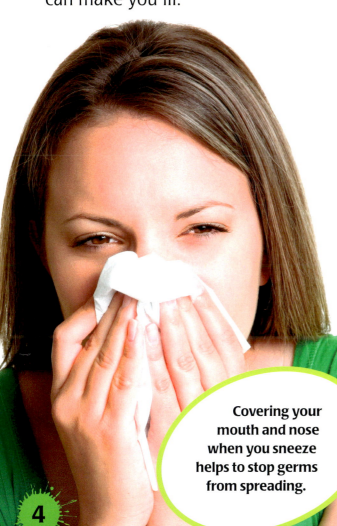

Covering your mouth and nose when you sneeze helps to stop germs from spreading.

Amazing fact

A sneeze comes out of your nose at 160 km per hour – faster than a car on the motorway! Sneezing spreads germs. Covering your mouth when you sneeze, and washing your hands afterwards, will help protect other people from catching your germs.

Contents

What is personal hygiene?   4

Looking after your hair   6

Healthy ears   8

Cleaning teeth   10

Hand care   12

Foot care   14

Skin care   16

A smelly body   18

For girls   20

For boys   22

What you wear   24

What you touch   26

Personal hygiene rota   28

Quiz   29

Glossary   30

Find out more   31

Index   32

Puberty

As you go through puberty and you grow from being a child into an adult, your body starts to change. Puberty releases a lot of different hormones, so all the necessary changes to your body can happen.

Some of these hormones make your skin and hair more oily and make your body smell more. This is all perfectly normal and everyone – even celebrities and pop stars – goes through the same thing. Good personal hygiene during puberty will help to keep you feeling fresh, and looking clean and healthy.

Your skin produces more oil during puberty, so it is important to keep It clean.

Looking after your hair

One of the first things that people notice is your hair. Looking after your hair helps you to look and feel your best. It is an important part of personal hygiene.

Washing hair

Everyone needs to wash their hair. Some people need to wash it often – perhaps every day or every two days, especially during puberty. You should always wash your hair at least once a week. This helps to get rid of the oil and dirt that builds up on it as you go through your daily life. Washing your hair makes it look clean and at its best.

Shampoo is the best product to use when washing hair. Do not be tempted to use soap or washing-up liquid instead. This will dry out your hair and can leave it in very poor condition. Instead, choose a shampoo that is good for your type of hair. Some people have naturally frizzy hair and special shampoo for dry or frizzy hair can help keep it under control. If your hair is very oily, choose a shampoo for greasy hair.

Keeping brushes clean will keep your hair cleaner, too.

You may wish to use hair conditioner after rinsing out shampoo. This will help to keep your hair soft and looking good. It will also make long hair easier to comb or brush. As with shampoos, choose a conditioner that is right for your hair type.

Head lice

Lice are tiny insects that can live in people's hair and on their scalp. They bite the scalp, and make it sore and itchy. Most people have head lice at some time in their lives. They are most common during school years. Do not worry if you get head lice, you can buy special products, which will soon get rid of them.

Head lice can crawl across hair onto someone else's head.

Healthy Hints

Dandruff busting

If you have dandruff, use special dandruff shampoo and conditioner. That way, your head will not feel itchy and you will avoid having little white specks on your clothes.

Healthy ears

You do not need to do much to look after your ears. However, a little ear care is all part of good personal hygiene.

Cleaning your ears

When you have a shower, bath or wash, clean the area behind your ears with soap. You do not need to wash inside your ears. Ear wax does this job for you. If your ears get wet inside, dry them gently with a towel but never push the towel right inside your ears, because you can easily damage them.

Cotton buds

Never use a cotton bud to try to get rid of ear wax. If you push it, or if it slips, too far into your ear, you can damage the eardrum. This can be very painful.

Ear wax

Ear wax is formed in the centre of your ear. It cleans your ears by working its way slowly out of your ears, taking with it any bits of dust or dirt. Ear wax also protects your ears. It helps to keep them free of infection and it keeps out tiny insects, too!

Sometimes, you can get a build-up of ear wax inside your ears. This can make it harder to hear clearly. Ear drops from a chemist's may help.

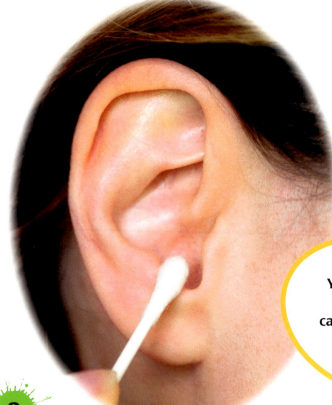

You can use a cotton bud to carefully clean the outer part of your ears.

Pierced ears

Some people like having pierced ears. It is best to have your ears pierced by somebody who has been properly trained and who is uses sterile equipment. If you pierce your own ears, you could get a serious infection.

Loud noise

Loud noise can damage your hearing. If you listen to very loud music, you may notice a ringing sound in your ears, or that your hearing sounds dull. This is a warning sign. Your hearing should return to normal very soon. However, if you regularly play music too loudly, you might damage your hearing permanently.

Avoid listening to very loud music, which can damage your hearing.

Cleaning teeth

An essential part of personal hygiene is looking after your teeth. Your teeth are very important; you need them for eating and speaking – and for that fabulous smile! It is very important keep your teeth clean and healthy.

Clean teeth, fresh breath

Your mouth is full of bacteria. Do not worry, this is perfectly normal. But this is why cleaning your teeth regularly is so important. Bacteria in your mouth produce a kind of acid, which can cause tooth decay. The bacteria also produce plaque, which can cause gum disease and make your breath smell bad.

Cleaning your teeth helps to clear away bacteria and plaque. You should clean your teeth at least twice a day – once in the morning and once before going to bed. If you can clean them more often than this, you will help your teeth to stay in tiptop condition.

Brushing your teeth twice a day will help to keep them strong.

Choose a toothbrush that has a small head and soft bristles. Toothbrushes with bristles that are different sizes are a good choice for extra-thorough cleaning. The toothbrush handle should be comfortable to hold.

To clean your teeth, put some toothpaste on your toothbrush, and use small circular movements to clean the front and back of all of your teeth. Make sure that you brush each one in turn. Spend at least three minutes cleaning your teeth. Spit out the toothpaste when you have finished brushing, but do not rinse out your mouth. Brush your tongue, too, to clear away bacteria. This will keep your breath fresh.

Dentist

Regular check-ups with a dentist help to keep your teeth and gums healthy. The dentist can spot any problems early on and can give you any treatment you need. Try to see a dentist every six months.

Healthy Hints

Sugar-free

To protect your teeth, cut back on the sugar you eat and drink. If you do eat or drink something sugary, try to brush your teeth afterwards, drink some water or chew sugar-free gum to clear away any sugar from your mouth.

If you do not clean your teeth regularly, you will end up with tooth decay.

Hand care

You use your hands all the time, and you touch many different things, from pens and plates to toys and toilets. Many of the things you touch have germs, which get onto your hands. Germs can cause illnesses, such as a sore throat, a cold or an upset tummy. To protect yourself from illnesses like these, you need to wash your hands regularly.

When to wash hands

Washing your hands is an important part of personal hygiene. You should always remember to wash your hands before you prepare food or eat a meal. Handwashing after using the toilet is essential, too.

If you are ill, you should wash your hands often – for example, after you cough. Always wash your hands before and after visiting someone who is ill, too. And, if you cut yourself, your hands need to be clean before you put on a plaster.

Amazing fact

The number of germs on your fingertips doubles after you use the toilet.

Washing your hands after using the toilet is an important part of personal hygiene.

Biting your nails is unsightly – and unhealthy!

When you have been playing outside, wash your hands to clean away any germs you may have picked up from the park or a football, for example. Do the same if you have been stroking an animal, such as a dog. Rubbish has got lots of germs on it! If you touch rubbish, washing your hands is extra-important.

How to wash hands

Wash your hands using soap and warm, running water. Work the soap into a lather on both sides of your hands, between your fingers, and under and around your nails. Do not forget your wrists. Rub your hands together for up to 20 seconds. Then rinse your hands with clean water, and dry them thoroughly with a clean towel, paper towel or hand dryer.

Nail biting

Some people bite their nails. This can make your nails look unsightly and can also make you ill if there are any germs on your hands. Try not to bite your nails. If you cannot stop, you can apply a special product to your nails, which tastes horrible, to put you off.

Foot care

Your feet are a perfect place for germs to grow, because wearing shoes, boots and trainers keeps them warm and damp – or even hot and sweaty. Bacteria love sweat and they make your feet smell. Good personal hygiene includes making sure that you take care of your feet. This helps you to feel fresh and clean.

Sweet-smelling feet!

The best way to keep your feet smelling sweet and feeling fresh is to wash them when you have a bath or shower. Do not forget to wash between your toes. Make sure that you dry your feet properly before you put on your socks and shoes. This will keep bacteria at bay.

Some kinds of socks and shoes are better than others. Cotton or wool socks, and leather shoes allow your feet to breathe more easily, so they are less likely to get hot and sweaty. Plastic shoes do not let your feet breathe, so they are not a good idea for everyday wear.

Remember to change your socks daily.

Changing your socks and shoes each day is a good personal hygiene habit. Socks are easy to change and wash. If you have more than just one pair of shoes, wear a different pair each day. Then, your other shoes have time to dry out. You can buy shoes that have insoles that can be washed. You can also buy special insoles to put in your shoes stop your feet smelling bad.

Foot conditions

Foot conditions, such as athlete's foot and verrucas, can be extremely uncomfortable. You can get and pass on athlete's foot and verrucas by walking around barefoot. However, these conditions are easy to treat. Keeping your feet clean and dry, and wearing socks and shoes, can help you to avoid picking them up.

Foot verrucas are caused by a virus. They can be quite painful.

Healthy Hints

Keep it short

Help to care for your feet by keeping your toenails short. Always cut your toenails straight across, to avoid in-grown toenails. This is when the nail grows into the skin, and it can be very painful.

Skin care

Your skin's main job is to keep germs out of your body and keep you free from illness. Looking after your skin, as part of your personal hygiene plan, will help it to do its job.

Washing your face

Everybody gets spots, especially during puberty. You might get just one or two spots but, sometimes, spots may be more of a problem. You can reduce the chance of getting spots by washing your face twice a day, to remove any dirt and germs. This will help to give you confidence, too, because you know that your face looks clean.

There are lots of products that you can use to clean your face, including soap, facial gels and cleansers. It is best to use a product that is mild, so your skin does not dry out. Wash your face using warm − not hot − water. If your skin feels very dry, try using a gentle moisturising lotion afterwards. This will make your skin feel softer.

Special cleansers can help to keep you spot-free.

Acne trouble

Some people develop acne during puberty. Acne is most common between the ages of 13 and 18. Puberty hormones cause the skin to produce an oily substance, called sebum. Sebum and dirt can block the skin's pores, causing acne. Acne can make people's skin feel very sore.

There is a lot that can be done to treat acne. Often, it goes away in its own time. However, it may last for a while. If you are at all worried about acne, your doctor can give you special medication to treat it.

In the sun

For the best protection, use a sunscreen with a Sun Protection Factor (SPF) rating of 15 or higher.

Sun screen

The sun is extremely strong. It can burn your skin, making it very sore. It is important to protect your skin from sunburn. To do this, it is best to stay out of direct sunshine between 11 am and 3 pm. When it is very sunny, cover up with a T-shirt and hat.

Always apply sunscreen to protect your skin from burning.

A smelly body

When you reach puberty, you may notice that your body starts to smell a little more than usual. For example, if you have been playing sport or running around a lot, your feet, around your groin, or under your arms may have quite a strong smell. This is called body odour. It happens when you sweat.

Do not worry about body odour; it is a perfectly normal part of growing up. It is simply caused by the changes in your hormone levels as you start to become an adult.

Sweat and body odour

Sweat is your body's natural way of cooling down when you are hot. Sometimes, people also sweat if they feel very nervous. As you get older, your sweat starts to smell more. In fact, the smell is caused by bacteria that live on your skin and feed off the sweat. It is the bacteria that smell, not the sweat.

Having a shower or bath after exercising will get rid of body odour.

Some people's sweat has a very mild smell or none at all. Other people have much stronger-smelling sweat. The good news is that there is a lot you can do to tackle body odour problems.

Preventing body odour

You can help to prevent body odour by having a shower or a bath regularly, and especially after exercise. You should shower or bathe in water that is warm, rather than hot. There are lots of different soaps, shower gels and bubble baths, which make you smell nice. However, all you really need is a mild soap, which will clean away all the sweat and dirt from your body.

You can choose from lots of different deodorants and antiperspirants.

Healthy Hints

Use deodorant

Underarm deodorant or antiperspirant can help with body odour. A deodorant hides the smell of sweat by covering it up with a fragrance. An antiperspirant stops you sweating or dries up sweat.

For girls

One of the big changes puberty brings for girls is having periods. A girl can start her periods any time between the age of nine and 17. There is no right or wrong time for periods to start – they begin exactly when the body is ready. Personal hygiene is especially important for girls and women during their period.

What is a period?

Women's bodies all have eggs, which can develop into babies when they are fertilised by sperm from men's bodies. Eggs are stored inside a woman's ovaries. Once a month, an ovary releases an egg. If the egg is fertilised, it travels to the woman's uterus, where it can develop into a baby. The uterus fills with blood to nourish the growing egg.

If the egg is not fertilised, the woman has a period. During her period, the blood from the uterus flows out of her body. A period normally lasts between three and seven days.

Being active can make you feel better during your period.

Sanitary towels and tampons

During a period, women wear a sanitary towel or tampon to absorb the blood. There are lots to choose from. You may feel more comfortable if you use a sanitary towel at first. Tampons are especially useful for going swimming when you cannot wear a sanitary towel.

Feminine hygiene

It is important to change sanitary towels or tampons regularly throughout your period. Changing every two to four hours is a good idea. This will keep you feeling clean and comfortable.

Showering or bathing every day will help you to feel fresher. Remember to wash using warm, rather than hot, water and use a gentle soap. During your period, you may want to have a shower or bath more often than usual.

Period pain

Some girls and women have period pains during their period. They may have a back ache or a tummy ache. They can ease the discomfort by putting a heat pad on their back or tummy.

A period may last up to seven days. Period pain can be uncomfortable.

For boys

Like girls, boys experience a lot of changes during puberty. For example, puberty hormones change a boy's voice and make it much deeper. The hormones make the hair on his body – for example, on his arms and legs – get thicker. They also make hair grow on parts of his body where there was no hair before, including under the (front of the) arms and on the face.

Facial hair is thin and soft at first, but it gets thicker over time. Towards the end of puberty, many boys decide to shave their facial hair. Shaving is part of a personal hygiene routine for many boys and men.

How often do you need to shave?

Some people shave more often than others. How often you need to shave depends on how fast your facial hair grows. Many people shave once a day, but some choose to grow a beard or to leave stubble instead.

As you get older, shaving will become part of your personal hygiene routine.

Shaving creams, gels and razors

You need to use special shaving creams or shaving gels and razors, for shaving. Shaving creams and gels help to soften your skin and make it easier for the razor to slide over it. The razor does the job of cutting the facial hair, leaving your face looking and feeling smooth and clean.

Boys can choose from lots of kinds of razors, including electric razors, disposable razors and razors with disposable blades. Remember, the most important thing is to choose a razor that has a clean, sharp blade, to cut quickly and easily through hair.

In your own time

Some boys worry that they do not need to shave when their friends have started shaving. Everyone is different, and people go through the different stages of puberty at different times. This is perfectly normal, so do not worry. There is no need to compare yourself with anyone else.

Regular showers will help to keep you clean and smelling fresh.

Amazing fact

An average hair grows about 1.5 cm every month.

What you wear

Personal hygiene involves keeping yourself clean. It is about looking after yourself. The clothes you wear can make a difference to how you feel. If your clothes are clean, that should help you to feel good about yourself and the way you look.

Keeping clothes clean

Clothes can become stained and dirty from day-to-day activities. They may get smelly, too, as your body produces more sweat during puberty. You can stay fresh-smelling and clean-looking by washing your clothes regularly. When you get home from school, hang up your school clothes to freshen them, ready for the next day.

It is especially important to wash your sports clothes after you have used them. Physical activity makes you sweat more and some of this sweat will be absorbed by your clothes, making them smell. If you leave damp, sweaty clothes in your sports bag, they can get musty and even grow mould.

Sports clothes need a good wash before you use them again!

Underwear

Some parts of your body, such as under your arms, are sweatier than others. Your underwear is right next to your skin, so it can get much more smelly than other clothes. Changing your underwear every day will help you to feel fresh and clean.

Remember your feet!

Sweat from your feet gets into your shoes and can make them very smelly. It is a good idea to change out of school shoes as soon as you get home. Remember to use different shoes on different days, if you can. This gives the shoes you have worn time to dry out and helps to prevent smells you want to avoid.

Amazing fact

Scientists in the United States of America are working on creating self-cleaning clothes. They are trying to blend fabric with bacteria that eat human sweat. If this works, one day, you will no longer need to wash your shirt to keep it clean!

Wearing clean clothes can give you confidence because you know that you look and feel fresh.

What you touch

Personal hygiene is mainly about caring for your body. However, it is also important to think about how hygienic the things around you are. If items, such as computer keyboards and telephones, are not kept clean, they can carry a lot of germs. When you touch them, some of these germs may get onto your body. If this happens, the germs may make you ill.

Germs, germs all around!

Some of the common items you use in a day are dirtier than you think. Keyboards on office computers have been shown to contain lots of germs and even bits of cornflakes and boiled sweets. It is best to avoid eating at your computer, especially if other people use it, too.

Amazing fact

There are about 400 times more bacteria on an average office keyboard as there are on a toilet seat.

Keeping your phone clean and germ-free will help you to catch fewer bugs.

It is a good idea to clean your computer keyboard once every three months.

Telephones, especially public ones, can be even dirtier than computer keyboards. People may use the phone while they are ill with a cold or flu, for example. If they cough or sneeze, their germs get onto the phone. The next person who uses the phone can pick up these germs. If that person touches their mouth, nose or eyes, the germs can get into their body.

Squeaky clean

You can keep a telephone and the outside of a computer keyboard clean by wiping over the surfaces with a clean, damp (not wet) cloth.

Vacuuming a computer keyboard picks up dirt that falls down between the buttons. You need to be really careful not to damage your computer, however, so always ask permission before you do any vacuuming.

Every surface you touch may carry germs. A few germs will not normally do you any harm, but sometimes they can make you unwell. You can help to prevent germs spreading, though. Make sure that you wash your hands whenever you go to the toilet. Also wash your hands after a job such as taking out the rubbish.

Personal hygiene rota

Personal hygiene is important for everyone. It keeps you looking and feeling your best.

Bathroom sharing

In your family, you probably share a bathroom, so it can be a good idea to have a bathroom rota. That way everyone in the family knows when it is their turn to use the bathroom and how long they can have. This can be especially helpful on busy mornings before people go to school or work.

Everyone's needs

Think about the needs of the people in the house. For example, who leaves the house first? Does anyone prefer to have a shower or bath in the evening?

Ask people how long they need in the bathroom, so you can try to give each person enough time. Try to organise your rota so that while someone is eating breakfast another person is using the bathroom. The bathroom will then be free for the person who has just eaten to clean his or her teeth.

Here is an example of a bathroom rota. You can use it as a starting point for creating your own rota.

Time	Mum	Dad	Charlie
7:00 am	Shower		Wash face and clean teeth
7:15 am			
7:30 am		Wash face, shave and clean teeth	

Quiz

How good are your personal hygiene habits? Try this quick quiz to find out!

1 **Your mum asks you to take the rubbish out before eating dinner. Do you:**

a) Take the rubbish out, then rush to the table; you're starving?

b) Take the rubbish out, then wash your hands with warm water and soap?

c) Take the rubbish out, then wipe your hands on your clothes?

2 **Your scalp feels really itchy and sore. Do you:**

a) Ignore it; it's probably nothing?

b) Tell your parents or caregivers; you may need treatment for head lice?

c) Wash your hair every day, and hope it gets better?

3 **Your ears feel a bit blocked, and you can't hear as well as usual. Do you:**

a) Stick a cotton bud in your ears, to try to get rid of any ear wax?

b) Ask your parents or caregivers if you need to use ear drops or see a doctor?

c) Not tell anyone; it may be a cold, and it will go away on its own?

4 **You buy a new pair of shoes. Do you:**

a) Wear them every day; they're your favourites?

b) Wear another pair of shoes every other day, so your new ones stay fresh and clean?

c) Wear them as much as you like; they aren't plastic, so they won't get smelly?

5 **You share a computer with your brother or sister. Do you:**

a) Use the computer as much as you can – even when you're eating a snack?

b) Clean the keyboard and mouse regularly, so no one picks up any germs?

c) Never clean the computer – your brother or sister can do it?

Mostly **bs**: Well done! You have learned a lot about the different aspects of personal hygiene. This will help to stay clean and healthy – and feel confident!

Mostly **as** or **cs**: Your personal hygiene habits still need a little work. Don't worry – you can do it! Keep reading this book; it will give you lots of ideas!

Glossary

antiperspirant A substance that is put on the skin, especially under the arms, to prevent sweating.

athlete's foot A fungal skin infection of the feet.

bacteria Organisms that can spread disease.

body odour An unpleasant smell on the body, caused by sweat.

dandruff Small, white bits of dead skin from the scalp, which gather in the hair or fall on clothes.

deodorant A substance that is put on the skin, especially under the arms, to hide smells.

disposable Something designed to be thrown away after use.

eardrum A membrane in the ear that vibrates when sounds reach it.

ear wax The soft, yellowish substance inside your ears.

eggs Cells in a woman's body, from which babies might develop if the eggs join with a sperm from a man.

fertilised When the man's sperm joins with a woman's egg.

germs Organisms that can spread disease.

groin The place where your trunk meets the top of your legs.

hormones Chemicals that tell the body to do certain things.

hygienic Clean and healthy.

insoles pieces of material that fit inside shoes and absorb sweat.

lather A mass of bubbles created when soap is mixed with water.

ovary Female reproductive organs that produce and release eggs.

plaque A white, sticky substance inside your mouth, caused by bacteria.

pores Very small holes in the skin.

sanitary towel A piece of soft, absorbent material worn by women between their legs during their period.

sebum An oily substance that keeps the skin and hair waterproof and stretchy.

sperm A cell in a man's body. If a sperm joins with an egg cell from a woman, a baby can develop.

sterile Clean and free from germs.

tampon A small cylinder of cotton or other material that fits inside a woman's body during her period.

tooth decay Small holes in your teeth. Tooth decay can be painful.

uterus The part of a woman's body where a baby develops before birth. It is also called the womb.

verrucas Small growths on the skin, usually on the bottom of the foot, caused by a viral infection.

Find out more

Books

My Health: What are Germs?
Silverstein *et al.*
(Franklin Watts, 2002)

Health Choices: Keeping Clean
Cath Senker
(Wayland, 2007)

Keeping Healthy: Personal Hygiene.
Carol Ballard
(Wayland, 2007)

My Healthy Body: Skin, Hair and Hygiene
Jen Green
(Franklin Watts 2008)

Websites

This website is full of information about your body and how to look after yourself.
http://kidshealth.org/kid/

For lots more information about personal hygiene, see:
www.cyh.sa.gov.au

This website has lots of information about puberty, including interactive images that show how boys' and girls' bodies change during puberty.
www.bbc.co.uk/science/human body/body/index.shtml?lifecycle

Index

acne 17
animals 13
antiperspirants 19

bacteria 4, 10, 11, 14, 18, 25
body hair 22
body smell 4, 14, 18–19
boys 22–23
breath 10, 11

cleansers 16
clothes 4, 24–25, 29
computer keyboard 4, 26, 27, 29
cuts 12

dandruff 7
dentist 11
deodorants 19
doctor 17, 29

ears 8–9, 29
eggs 20

feet 14–15, 25

germs 4, 12, 13, 14, 16, 26, 27
girls 20–21
gums 11

hair 5, 6–7
hands 12–13
head lice 7, 29
hearing 8, 9
hormones 5, 17, 18, 22

illness 4, 12, 16, 26
infection 4, 8, 9

nails 13, 15

ovaries 20

periods 20–21
pierced ears 9
plaque 10
puberty 5, 6, 16, 17, 18, 20, 22, 23, 24

rubbish 13, 27, 29

sanitary towels 21
sebum 17
shampoo 6, 7
shaving 22–23
skin 5, 16–17, 18, 23
sneezing 4, 27
soap 13, 16, 19
sperm 20
spots 4, 16
sunburn 17
sweat 14, 18–19, 24, 25

tampons 21
teeth 10–11
telephones 26, 27
toilet 4, 12, 26, 27
tongue 11
tooth decay 10, 11

uterus 20

voice 22